HE GETS US

Experiencing the confounding love,
forgiveness, and relevance of Jesus

With selections from the writings of
MAX LUCADO

THOMAS NELSON
Since 1798

He Gets Us

© 2023 He Gets Us

This book is a compilation of excerpts from the following:

3:16, 97814002330, 2007, 2022, Max Lucado. *And the Angels Were Silent*, 9780849947513, 1987, Max Lucado. *Anxious for Nothing*, 9780718096120, 2017, Max Lucado. *God's Story, Your Story*, 9780310294030, 2011, Max Lucado. *Jesus*, 9781400214693, 2020, Max Lucado. *Just Like Jesus*, 9780849917851, 1998, 2003, Max Lucado. *No Wonder They Call Him Savior*, 9780849947117, 1986, 2004, Max Lucado. *On Calvary's Hill*, 9780718031329, 2013, Max Lucado. *Six Hours One Friday*, 9781400207404, 1989, 2004, Max Lucado.

Published in Nashville, Tennessee, by Thomas Nelson. Thomas Nelson is a registered trademark of HarperCollins Christian Publishing, Inc.

Thomas Nelson titles may be purchased in bulk for educational, business, fund-raising, or sales promotional use. For information, please email SpecialMarkets@ThomasNelson.com.

Unless otherwise noted, Scripture quotations are taken from the Holy Bible, New International Version®, NIV®. Copyright © 1973, 1978, 1984, 2011 by Biblica, Inc.® Used by permission of Zondervan. All rights reserved worldwide. www.zondervan.com. The "NIV" and "New International Version" are trademarks registered in the United States Patent and Trademark Office by Biblica, Inc.®

Scripture quotations marked ESV are taken from the ESV® Bible (The Holy Bible, English Standard Version®). Copyright © 2001 by Crossway, a publishing ministry of Good News Publishers. Used by permission. All rights reserved. Scripture quotations marked THE MESSAGE are taken from The Message. Copyright © 1993, 2002, 2018 by Eugene H. Peterson. Used by permission of NavPress. All rights reserved. Represented by Tyndale House Publishers, a Division of Tyndale House Ministries. Scripture quotations marked NASB are taken from the New American Standard Bible® (NASB). Copyright © 1960, 1962, 1963, 1968, 1971, 1972, 1973, 1975, 1977, 1995, 2020 by The Lockman Foundation. Used by permission. www.Lockman.org. Scripture quotations marked NCV are taken from the New Century Version®. Copyright © 2005 by Thomas Nelson. Used by permission. All rights reserved. Scripture quotations marked NKJV are taken from the New King James Version®. Copyright © 1982 by Thomas Nelson. Used by permission. All rights reserved. Scripture quotations marked RSV are taken from the Revised Standard Version of the Bible. Copyright © 1946, 1952, and 1971 National Council of the Churches of Christ in the United States of America. Used by permission. All rights reserved. Scripture quotations marked THE VOICE are taken from The Voice™. Copyright © 2012 by Ecclesia Bible Society. Used by permission. All rights reserved.

Cover Design: Grace Cavalier
Interior Design: Emily Ghattas

ISBN 978-1-4003-3892-4 (audiobook)
ISBN 978-1-4003-3891-7 (eBook)
ISBN 978-1-4041-1935-2 (paperback)

Library of Congress Cataloging-in-Publication Data on File

Printed in the United States of America

22 23 24 25 26 LBC 5 4 3 2 1

"From the beginning, we've wanted to share the real Jesus of the Bible."

—*He Gets Us*

Contents

Part 3: Hope

Part 4: Activism & Justice

Introduction

He Gets Us is a movement to reintroduce people to the Jesus of the Bible and his confounding love and forgiveness. We believe his words, example, and life have relevance in our lives today and offer hope for a better future.

This movement started with a diverse group of people passionate about the authentic Jesus of the Bible. While much has been said about him, much is still misunderstood. But we're confident that as people read, learn, and clearly understand for themselves who Jesus is, they'll find wisdom, hope, and peace unlike any other offered.

Be assured, though, that we're not "*left*" or "*right*" or a political organization of any kind. We're also not affiliated with any particular church or denomination.

We simply want everyone to understand the authentic Jesus as he's depicted in the Bible—the Jesus of radical forgiveness, compassion, and love.

It isn't hard to guess that we're led by Jesus fans and followers. People who believe he was much more than just a good guy and a profound teacher. And that Jesus is the Son of God, who came to earth, died, and was resurrected, then returned to heaven and is alive today.

We also have included many voices in our work here—welcoming diverse perspectives, backgrounds, and experiences to help us address the many concerns and issues we all face.

Our hope is that you see how Jesus experienced challenges and emotions just as we do. We want to provide a safe place to ask questions, including the tough ones.

We are also about sharing Jesus' openness to people who others might have excluded. His message went out to all. And though you may see religious people as often hypocritical or judgmental, know that Jesus saw that too—and didn't like it either. Instead, Jesus taught and offered radical compassion and stood up for the marginalized.

We hope this book serves as a resource for answering questions you have about Jesus and his love for each of us. Each chapter begins with content from the contributors of He Gets Us and is followed by a QR code to a video that provides a modern-day visual on the topic. Next we've included selected writings from *New York Times* bestselling author Max Lucado. His teachings offer valuable insight on answers to the most frequently asked questions people have about Jesus. At the end of each chapter, you'll find Scripture verses that specifically highlight answers to the question.

Ultimately, we want people to know Jesus' teachings and how he lived while here on earth. And this will be a starting point to understanding him and his message. Though we believe he was what Christians call fully God and fully man, that may not be what you believe. We're simply inviting you to explore with us at He Gets Us how might things be different if more people followed his example and his message. So look at this as an open invitation to engage and learn more. We're also here to support and listen to you.

Connect with us here:

Part 1

Real Life

Chapter 1

Was Jesus ever stressed?

Writings from He Gets Us

One night he experienced overwhelming stress because he knew he'd soon face arrest, torture, and even execution. It created an unimaginable weight.

Like many people do when stressed, Jesus escaped to a quiet place—a garden of old-growth olive trees on the side of a mountain. He brought a few friends for emotional support and prayer. Overwhelmed with exhaustion, his friends couldn't stay awake as Jesus pleaded with God for another way. But he knew there was no way around this moment; he needed to bear this cross.

Jesus said his soul was grieved to the point of death—that's how he described the stress he felt. He reportedly suffered hematohidrosis, a rare condition caused by acute emotional stress where the sweat glands rupture, causing them to excrete blood. He was clearly challenged by what he was facing even while knowing that his death would show his love and would change the world.

His adversaries captured him later that evening in the garden. Yet Jesus found the strength to face his accusers and submit to them willingly and without violence, knowing that his death would further spread his message of radical love.

Writings from Max Lucado

Our world is stressed. Jesus gets that. He faced the issues we face and some far more severe than we ever will. He taught how to deal with the challenges of life. And the key to what he taught is to believe God cares for you. Jesus starts by addressing our belief systems. Your belief system has nothing to do with your skin color, appearance, talents, or age. Your belief system is not concerned with the exterior of the tent but the interior. It is the set of convictions (poles)—all of them unseen—upon which your faith depends. If your belief system is strong, you will stand. If it is weak, the storm will prevail.

Belief always precedes behavior. For this reason the apostle Paul in each of his epistles addressed convictions before he addressed actions. To change the way a person responds to life, change what a person believes about life. The most important thing about you is your belief system.

Paul's was Gibraltar strong.

Take a close look at the poles in the tent of the apostle, and you will see one with this inscription: the sovereignty of God. *Sovereignty* is the term the Bible uses to describe God's perfect control and management of the universe. He preserves and governs every element. He is continually involved with all created things, directing them to act in a way that fulfills his divine purpose.

In the treatment of anxiety, a proper understanding of sovereignty is huge. Anxiety is often the consequence of perceived chaos. If we sense we are victims of unseen, turbulent, random forces, we are troubled.

Psychologists learned something fascinating about belief systems when they studied the impact of combat on soldiers in World War II. They determined that after sixty days of continuous combat the ground troops became "emotionally dead." This reaction is understandable. Soldiers endured a constant threat of bomb blitzes, machine guns, and enemy snipers. The anxiety of ground troops was no surprise.

The comparative calm of fighter pilots, however, was. Their mortality rate was among the highest in combat. Fifty percent of them were killed in action, yet dogfighters loved their work. An astounding 93 percent of them claimed to be happy in their assignments even though the odds of survival were the same as the toss of a coin.[1]

What made the difference? Those pilots had their hands on the throttle. They sat in the cockpit. They felt that their fate was theirs to determine.[2] Infantrymen, by contrast, could just as easily be killed standing still or running away. They felt forlorn and helpless. The formula is simple: Perceived control creates calm. Lack of control gives birth to fear.

You don't need a war to prove this formula. Road congestion will do just fine. A team of German researchers found that a traffic jam increases your chances of a heart attack threefold.[3] Makes sense. Gridlock is the ultimate loss of control. We may know how to drive, but that fellow in the next lane doesn't! We can be the best drivers in history, but the texting teenager might be the end of us. There is no predictability, just stress. Anxiety increases as perceived control diminishes.

So what do we do?

Control everything? Never board a plane without a parachute. Never enter a restaurant without bringing our own clean silverware. Never leave the house without a gas mask. Never give away our heart for fear of a broken one. Never step on a crack lest we break our mother's back. Face anxiety by taking control.

If only we could.

Yet certainty is a cruel impostor. A person can accumulate millions of dollars and still lose it in a recession. A health fanatic can eat only nuts and veggies and still battle cancer. A hermit can avoid all human contact and still struggle with insomnia. We want certainty, but the only certainty is the lack thereof.

That's why the most stressed-out people are control freaks. They fail at the quest they most pursue. The more they try to control the world, the more they realize they cannot. Life becomes a cycle of anxiety, failure; anxiety, failure; anxiety, failure. We can't take control because control is not ours to take.

The Bible has a better idea. Rather than seeking total control, relinquish it. You can't run the world, but you can entrust it to God. This is the message behind Paul's admonition to "rejoice *in the Lord*" (Philippians 4:4). Peace is within reach, not for lack of problems but because of the presence of a sovereign Lord. Rather than rehearse the chaos of the world, rejoice in the Lord's sovereignty, as Paul did. "The things which happened to me have actually turned out for the furtherance of the gospel, so that it has become evident to the whole palace guard, and to all the rest, that my chains are in Christ" (Philippians 1:12–13 NKJV).

God's answer for troubled times has always been the same: heaven has an occupied throne. This was certainly the message God gave to the prophet Isaiah. During the eighth century BC, ancient Judah enjoyed a time of relative peace, thanks to the steady leadership of Uzziah, the king. Uzziah was far from perfect, yet he kept the enemies at bay. Though antagonists threatened from all sides, the presence of Uzziah kept the fragile society safe from attack for fifty-two years.

Then Uzziah died. Isaiah, who lived during the reign of the king, was left with ample reason for worry. What would happen to the people of Judah now that Uzziah was gone?

Or, in your case, what will happen now that your job is gone? Or your health has diminished? Or the economy has taken a nosedive? Does God have a message for his people when calamity strikes?

He certainly had a word for Isaiah. The prophet wrote:

> In the year that King Uzziah died, I saw the Lord sitting on a throne, high and lifted up, and the train of His robe filled the temple. Above it stood seraphim; each one had six wings: with two he covered his face, with two he covered his feet, and with two he flew. And one cried to another and said:
>
>> "Holy, holy, holy is the LORD of hosts;
>> The whole earth is full of His glory!"
>> (Isaiah 6:1–3 NKJV)

Uzziah's throne was empty, but God's was occupied. Uzziah's reign had ended, but God's had not. Uzziah's voice was silent, but God's was strong (Isaiah 6:8–10). He was, and is, alive, on the throne, and worthy of endless worship.

God calmed the fears of Isaiah, not by removing the problem but by revealing his divine power and presence.

Think of it this way. Suppose your dad is the world's foremost orthopedic surgeon. People travel from distant countries for him to treat them. Regularly he exchanges damaged joints for healthy ones. With the same confidence that a mechanic changes spark plugs, your dad removes and replaces hips, knees, and shoulders.

At ten years of age you are a bit young to comprehend the accomplishments of a renowned surgeon. But you're not too young to stumble down the stairs and twist your ankle. You roll and writhe on the floor and scream for help. You are weeks away from your first school dance. This is no time for crutches. No time for limping. You need a healthy ankle! Yours is anything but.

Into the room walks your dad, still wearing his surgical scrubs. He removes your shoe, peels back your sock, and examines the injury. You groan at the sight of the tennis ball–sized bump. Adolescent anxiety kicks in.

"Dad, I'll never walk again!"

"Yes, you will."

"No one can help me!"

"I can."

"No one knows what to do!"

"I do."

"No, you don't!"

Your dad lifts his head and asks you a question. "Do you know what I do for a living?"

Actually you don't. You know he goes to the hospital every day. You know that people call him "doctor." Your mom thinks he is smart. But you don't really know what your father does.

"So," he says as he places a bag of ice on your ankle, "it's time for you to learn." The next day he is waiting for you in the school parking lot after classes. "Hop in. I want you to see what I do," he says. He drives you to his hospital office and shows you the constellation of diplomas on his wall. Adjacent to them is a collection of awards that include words like *distinguished* and *honorable*. He hands you a manual of orthopedic surgery that bears his name.

"You wrote this?"

"I did."

His cell phone rings. After the call he announces, "We're off to surgery." You scrub up and follow him into the operating room on your crutches. During the next few hours you have a ringside seat for a procedure in which he reconstructs an ankle. He is the commandant of the operating room. He never hesitates or seeks advice. He just does it.

One of the nurses whispers, "Your dad is the best."

As the two of you ride home that evening, you look at your father. You see him in a different light. If he can conduct orthopedic surgery, he can likely treat a swollen ankle. So you ask, "You think I'll be okay for the dance?"

"Yes, you'll be fine."

This time you believe him. Your anxiety decreases as your understanding of your father increases.

Here is what I think: our biggest fears are sprained ankles to God.

Here is what else I think: a lot of people live with unnecessary anxiety over temporary limps.

The next time you fear the future, rejoice in the Lord's sovereignty. Rejoice in what he has accomplished. Rejoice that he is able to do what you cannot do. Fill your mind with thoughts of God.

"[He is] the Creator, who is blessed forever" (Romans 1:25 NKJV).

"[He] is the same yesterday, today, and forever"
(Hebrews 13:8 NKJV).

"[His] years will never end" (Psalm 102:27).

He is king, supreme ruler, absolute monarch, and overlord of all history.

An arch of his eyebrow and a million angels will pivot and salute. Every throne is a footstool to his. Every crown is papier-mâché next to his. He consults no advisers. He needs no congress. He reports to no one. He is in charge.

Sovereignty gives the saint the inside track to peace. Others see the problems of the world and wring their hands. We see the problems of the world and bend our knees.

Scripture reference: Romans 5:6–8

Chapter 2

What would Jesus think of teen moms?

Writings from He Gets Us

The story of Jesus' birth is told every year around Christmas. It's a familiar story, with familiar characters and setting: a stable, an innkeeper, a star, angels, shepherds, wise men, a baby in a manger, and a young couple.

Jesus was born to a teenage girl. A girl who was

scared and forced to travel far away from her home right before she gave birth. A girl who was at the mercy of a man who, in the culture of the times, could have publicly shamed her or even had her killed but who instead protected and supported her. A girl who gave birth in a stable because she had nowhere else to go.

The story of Jesus is also the story of that young girl. Imagine what that moment in time would've been like for her. The video below is a reminder that Jesus came to the world by way of a human mom. Jesus wasn't just a baby in a manger. His life was not some fairy tale—it was very real. His first few minutes in this world looked like anyone else's, crying in the arms of his mom. His teen mom.

Writings from Max Lucado

Why did God use Mary and Joseph? He didn't have to. He could have just laid the Savior on a doorstep. Would have been simpler that way. And why does God tell us their stories? Why does God give us an entire testament of the blunders and stumbles of his people?

Simple. He knew what you and I watched on the news last night. He knew you would fret. He knew I would worry. And he wants us to know that when the world goes wild, he stays calm.

Want proof? Before the Gospel of Matthew tells us about Mary, Joseph, and Jesus, Matthew listed a lengthy genealogy. In spite of all the crooked halos found on the list, the last name is the first one promised—Jesus.

"Joseph was the husband of Mary, and Mary was the mother of Jesus. Jesus is called the Christ" (Matthew 1:16 NCV).

Period. No more names are listed. No more are needed. As if God is announcing to a doubting world, "See, I did it. Just as I said I would. The plan succeeded."

The famine couldn't starve it.

Four hundred years of Egyptian slavery couldn't oppress it.

Wilderness wanderings couldn't lose it.

Babylonian captivity couldn't stop it.

Clay-footed pilgrims couldn't spoil it.

The promise of the Messiah threads its way through forty-two generations of rough-cut stones, forming a necklace fit for the King who came. Just as promised.

And the promise remains.

"Those people who keep their faith until the end will be saved," Joseph's child assured (Matthew 24:13 NCV).

Scripture references: Matthew 1:18–25; Luke 2:7

Chapter 3

Was Jesus ever lonely?

Writings from He Gets Us

Social distancing. It's one of the most common terms used during COVID-19. We started using a lot of terms we don't normally use, words like *pandemic*, *self-isolating*, and *quarantine*. But regardless of the words we use to describe our disruptive times, what too many of us experience is loneliness. Many of us went months without seeing our closest friends and loved ones, and we weren't sure when the separation would end.

Do you wonder whether Jesus ever experienced such loneliness? As a man who traveled throughout the land of his birth gathering fame and followers, he knew how it felt to be surrounded by loving company. But like us, he also knew how it felt to lose that love without warning.

During his lifetime Jesus watched thousands of his followers walk away. When he was being prosecuted unjustly, his closest friends abandoned him out of fear. As he awaited execution, he stood alone. And in his darkest moment, as he died on the cross, Jesus felt abandoned.

As we begin to emerge from the pandemic, the impact of isolation lingers. We feel it. We see it in our families, coworkers, and friends. But understanding Jesus' loneliness can be a comforting reminder . . . that even in isolation, we're not alone.

Writings from Max Lucado

Have you ever thought: *Who will love me? I feel so old. Unloved. Unwanted. Abandoned. I just want to cry and sleep forever* . . . Can you hear them? The divorcé. The abandoned child. The man after a one-night stand. The woman by a silent phone. Cries of loneliness.

No one knows that you are lonely. On the outside you are packaged perfectly. Your smile is quick. Your job is stable. Your clothes are sharp. Your waist is small. Your calendar is full. Your walk brisk. Your talk impressive. But when you look in the mirror, you fool no one. When you are alone, the duplicity ceases, and the pain surfaces.

Or maybe you don't try to hide it. Maybe you have always been outside the circle, looking in, and everyone knows it. Your conversation is a bit awkward. Your companionship is seldom requested. Your clothes are dull. Your looks are common. Ziggy is your hero, and Charlie Brown is your mentor.

Am I striking a chord? If I am, if you have nodded or sighed in understanding, I have an important message for you.

The most gut-wrenching cry of loneliness in history didn't come from a widow or a patient. It came from a hill, from a cross, from a Messiah. "My God, my God," Jesus screamed, "why have you abandoned me?" (Matthew 27:46 NCV).

I think of all the people who cast despairing eyes

toward the dark heavens and cry, "Why?" And I imagine him listening. I picture his eyes misting and a pierced hand brushing away a tear. He may offer no answer, he may solve no dilemma, but he who also was once alone—understands!

Scripture references: John 6:60–71; Matthew 26:69–75

Chapter 4

Can I judge without being judgmental?

Writings from He Gets Us

There's a scripture that kind of trips us up. Whether you're a Bible reader or not, you're probably familiar with it. "Do not judge, or you too will be judged" (Matthew 7:1). Jesus said this toward the end of one of his most famous sermons. He was calling out the hypocrisy of pointing out the faults in others when we have our own faults we should be working on.

But is it realistic to never judge anyone? There are times when judging is necessary. When applying for a job, it's natural to think, *Do I want to work for this person?* When meeting someone you're attracted to, *Should I ask them out on a date?* When you need to confide in someone, *Who do I trust as a friend?* Just spending a couple of minutes online, we realize our entire world is now based on reviews. From doctors to hotels, restaurants to dog walkers, many businesses live or die by the number of stars by their names. Honest evaluation of others is necessary for a safe and functioning society.

Honest evaluation, however, is not the judgment Jesus meant. The judging Jesus referred to comes from a different place. It comes from our egos, from seeking to elevate ourselves by belittling someone else. Or trying to justify our own bad behaviors by labeling somebody else's behavior as worse. Sometimes, biases and grudges affect how we view and treat others.

With that in mind, Jesus asked us to stop pinpointing the shortcomings of others and to look inwardly and deeply examine our own hearts and motives. It's not comfortable. But here's why it's so important: Jesus knew that if we focused on our own faults and weaknesses, we would become more empathetic toward others. We'd recognize that, like us, every person has challenges and struggles that we can relate to. And that's how Jesus' radical love is demonstrated today. By recognizing our own flaws, we can all become a little more merciful, a little more patient, and a little more loving toward one another.

Writings from Max Lucado

Judgmental people would ask, "Why deal with my mistakes when I can focus on the mistakes of others?"

They might follow up with internal struggles like *I may be bad, but as long as I can find someone worse, I am safe.* They fuel their goodness with the failures of others. They are the self-appointed teacher's pets in elementary school. They tattle on the sloppy work of others, oblivious to the F on their own papers. They are the neighborhood watchdogs, passing out citations for people to clean up their acts, never noticing the garbage on their own front lawns.

"Come on, God, let me show you the evil deeds of

my neighbor," the moralists invite. But God won't follow them into the valley. "If you think you can judge others, you are wrong. When you judge them, you are really judging yourself guilty, because you do the same things they do" (Romans 2:1 NCV). It's a shallow ploy, and God won't fall for it.

It is one thing to have a conviction; it's another to convict the person. Paul said in Romans 2:2: "God judges those who do wrong things, and we know that his judging is right" (NCV).

It's important to recognize the difference between honest evaluations and judgment—that is where the majority of misconceptions arise. You must know that you're not a sinner because you judged someone. Let's face it, we all do it more than we'd like to admit, but it's part of our makeup.

The Bible speaks about sin, how we miss the mark of God and his holy nature. We see the devastating effects of sin all around us every day. It is our job to hate the sin. But it is God's job to deal with the sinner. God has called us to despise evil, but he has never called us to despise the evildoer. But, oh, how we would like to! Is there any act more delightful than judging others? There's something smug and self-satisfying about slamming down the gavel . . . "Guilty!" Judging others is a quick and easy way to feel good about ourselves. But that's the problem. God doesn't compare us to them. They are not the standard. God is. And compared to him, Paul argued in Romans 3:12, "There is no one who does anything good" (NCV).

Scripture references: Matthew 7:1; Luke 6:37; John 7:24

Part 2

Struggle

Chapter 5

Did Jesus live in poverty?

Writings from He Gets Us

Jesus displayed immense empathy for the poor and the needy. But why? Then it struck us. He noted that birds had nests and foxes had holes, but he didn't have a place to rest his head each night. His life was one of simplicity and deprivation.

The man who prayed to God, "Give us this day our daily bread," experienced hunger. The man who offered "living water," ironically, knew thirst.

His life was not luxurious or easy. He labored with his hands. He didn't have a closet full of clothes or a pantry filled with food. He was a nomad relying on the kindness and generosity of others.

This was the Jesus that we knew so many could relate to. People struggling to pay the rent. Parents facing the dilemma of either going to an hourly wage job or staying home with a sick child. Hard workers holding two and three jobs just to fill gas tanks and refrigerators.

The exhaustion, the uncertainty, and the struggle are all things we have in common with the Jesus of two thousand years ago.

Writings from Max Lucado

Ordinary man. Ordinary place. But a conduit of extraordinary grace. And in God's story, ordinary matters.

Jesus was an ordinary baby. There is nothing in the story to imply that he levitated over the manger or walked out of the stable. Just the opposite. He "dwelt among us" (John 1:14 NKJV). John's word for *dwelt* traces its origin to *tabernacle* or *tent*. Jesus did not separate himself from his creation; he pitched his tent in the neighborhood.

The Word of God entered the world with the cry of a baby. His family had no cash or connections or strings to pull. Jesus, the Maker of the universe, the one who invented time and created breath, was born into a town so crowded they literally had to deliver the child in a stable.

Step into the stable, and cradle in your arms the infant Jesus, still moist from the womb, just wrapped in rags. Run a finger across his chubby cheek, and listen as one who knew him well puts lyrics to the event: "In the beginning was the Word" (John 1:1 NKJV).

The words "In the beginning" take us to the beginning. "In the beginning God created the heavens and the earth" (Genesis 1:1 NKJV). The baby Mary held was connected to the dawn of time. He saw the first ray of sunlight and heard the first crash of a wave. The baby was born, but the Word never was.

"All things were made through him" (1 Corinthians 8:6 NCV). Not by him but through him. Jesus didn't fashion the world out of raw material he found. He created all things out of nothing. He struggled just as we do. He experienced the same physical hardships of hunger, pain, and exhaustion. He experienced the same financial woes and concerns. He understands our struggles because of his own struggles.

Scripture references: Matthew 8:20; John 14: 1–3

Chapter 6

Why did Jesus Cry?

Writings from He Gets Us

We're people, like you. The past few years, especially, have affected each and every one of us. We've felt alone. We've felt trapped and afraid. We've lost loved ones. What in Jesus' teachings could possibly make any of that feel better? What could he have possibly said that would bring comfort or hope? The truth is, when his dearest friends lost someone they loved, he didn't say anything.

He wept. Sometimes, just being there and grieving with someone is all we can do.

Writings from Max Lucado

On Calvary's hill Jesus cried out in a loud voice and died. Then the curtain in the temple was torn into two pieces, from the top to the bottom. What did fifteen hundred years of a curtain-draped holy of holies communicate? Simple—God is holy!

God is holy, separate from us and unapproachable. Even Moses was told, "You cannot see my face, because no one can see me and live" (Exodus 33:20 NCV). God is holy, and we are sinners, and there's a distance between us. But Jesus hasn't left us with an unapproachable God. "There is one God and one Mediator between God and men, the Man Christ Jesus" (1 Timothy 2:5 NKJV).

When Jesus' flesh was torn on the cross, the curtain was torn in two. With no hesitation we are welcome into God's presence—any day, anytime. The barrier of sin is down. No more curtain.

But we have a tendency to put the barrier back up.

Though there is no curtain in a temple, there is a curtain in the heart. And sometimes—no, oftentimes—we allow our mistakes to create a barrier that keeps us from God. A guilty conscience becomes a curtain that separates us from God.

Scripture reference: John 11:32-37

Chapter 7

Did Jesus ever mourn?

Writings from He Gets Us

As the restrictions of the pandemic eased and the world appeared to be resuming some normalcy (whatever that is), the He Gets Us team chatted about the impact COVID-19 had on us. Some of the changes it created, we agreed, were positive—realigning priorities and work-life balances, for example. But we couldn't comprehend the grief, pain, and anguish millions had gone through with the loss of loved ones, friends, and coworkers.

Thousands had perished in isolation with nobody at their sides. Now add to that the caregivers who risked their health and lives to tend to those who were suffering, and the sorrow becomes incalculable. This was a global catastrophe, but it was experienced on an individual level. These losses were personal. They cut to the core of people's souls. The pandemic even made many question the existence of a God or why an all-loving, all-powerful being would allow this to happen. Difficult questions. And honestly, we didn't try to formulate any answers. Crises will always drive some to faith and others to skepticism.

But through the dialogue, we eventually recognized that Jesus, a man who lived two thousand years ago, also understood the depth of sorrow many of us, our families, and our friends had or are still going through today. When Jesus received the news that his cousin, John the Baptist, had been executed by King Herod, he departed by ship and fled to the desert to be alone and grieve. The New Testament merely touches on it in a single verse, but we imagine the sorrow was deep, excruciating, and very real.

When Jesus heard the news of his good friend Lazarus's death, he wept. The shortest verse in the Bible,

Matt 14:12,13

yet maybe the most revealing. "Jesus wept" (John 11:35). We're quite certain there were more. At his crucifixion, there's mention of his mother, Mary, but no mention of Joseph. One can assume he'd experienced the loss of a beloved father figure.

All of this led us to seek images powerful enough to reflect that heartbreak. Our ideas were merely on paper, so credit must be given to the artists that drew upon their personal experiences to bring this video to life. While curating these scenes, the emotions were palpable. Tears welled up in our own eyes. And we must acknowledge the skill and talent of the editor and music composers who wove the images and sound score into a tapestry of solemn beauty.

Hopefully, it will touch you as much as it's touched us.

Writings from Max Lucado

Mourning is not evidence of disbelief. Jesus experienced sorrow. He mourned. His own tears give you permission to shed your own. Grieving and mourning don't mean you lack trust in God. They just mean you're human, with human emotions. Yet the fear of death has filled a thousand prisons. You can't see the walls. You can't see the warden. You can't see the locks. But you can see the prisoners. You can see them as they sit on their bunks and bemoan their fate. They want to live, but they can't because they are doomed to do what they most want to avoid—they will die. Imagine Jesus seeing us in our "prisons" of fear:

Jesus' throat tightened as he walked among the inmates. He gazed at the chalky faces through watery eyes. How long would they listen to Satan's lies? How long would they be in bondage? What would he have to do to convince them? Hadn't he proved it at Nain? Was the raising of Jairus's daughter not proof enough? How long would these people lock themselves into this man-made prison of fear? He had shown them the key to unlock their doors. Why didn't they use it?

"Show me the tomb."

They led him to the burial place of Lazarus. It was a cave with a stone laid across the entrance. Over the stone was spun the spiderweb of finality. "No more!" the stone boasted. "No more shall these hands move. No longer shall this tongue speak. No more!"

Jesus wept. He wept not for the dead but for the living. He wept not for the one in the cave of death but for those in

the cave of fear. He wept for those who, though alive, were
dead. He wept for those who, though free, were prisoners,
held captive by their fear of death.

"Move the stone." The command was soft but firm.

"But, Jesus, it will . . . it will stink."

"Move the stone so you will see God."

He called Lazarus out of the grave of death. And he calls us out of the grave of sorrow. Stones have never stood in God's way. *Thank you, Jesus!*

Scripture references: Matthew 14:6–14;
John 11:17–44; Matthew 26:36–46

Part 3

Hope

Chapter 8

Did Jesus
have fun?

Writings from He Gets Us

From the beginning, we've wanted to share the real Jesus.
At some point along the way, we realized that despite
our best efforts to show a true and complete picture of
him, that image became a bit unbalanced. Not incor-
rect but incomplete. We spent so much time reflecting
on heavier topics that when we stepped back to look at
the whole mosaic, we couldn't help but notice we were
showing a picture of Jesus that was distinctly lacking joy.

This video is a response to that—a sort of rebalancing. As it turns out, Jesus was no stranger to joy. He went to weddings. He shared lively meals with his friends. He drank with them. He had so much fun and acted so freely around the dinner table, the uptight religious leaders called him a glutton and a drunkard (Matthew 11:19). He didn't worry about what would happen to his reputation when he hung out with people who others thought were shady, and he was always uninhibited in his pursuit of compassion and joy for others. Jesus let his hair down too.

Writings from Max Lucado

I have a sketch of Jesus laughing. It hangs on the wall across from my desk.

It's quite a drawing. His head is back. His mouth is open. His eyes are sparkling. He isn't just grinning. He isn't just chuckling. He's roaring. He hasn't heard or seen something like that in quite a while. He's having trouble catching his breath.

It was given to me by an Episcopal priest who carries

cigars in his pocket and collects portraits of Jesus smiling. "I give them to anyone who might be inclined to take God too seriously," he explained as he handed me the gift.

He pegged me well.

I'm not one who easily envisions a smiling God. A weeping God, yes. An angry God, okay. A mighty God, you bet. But a chuckling God? It seems too . . . too . . . too unlike what God should do—and be. Which just shows how much I know—or don't know—about God.

What do I think he was doing when he stretched the neck of the giraffe? An exercise in engineering? What do I think he had in mind when he told the ostrich where to put his head? Spelunking? What do I think he was doing when he designed the mating call of an ape? Or the eight legs of the octopus? And what do I envision on his face when he saw Adam's first glance at Eve? A yawn?

Hardly.

As my vision improves and I'm able to read without my stained glasses, I'm seeing that a sense of humor is perhaps the only way God has put up with us for so long.

Is that God with a smile as Moses does a double take at the burning bush that speaks?

Is he smiling again as Jonah lands on the beach, dripping gastric juices and smelling like whale breath?

Is that a twinkle in his eye as he watches the disciples feed thousands with one boy's lunch?

Do you think his face is deadpan as he speaks about the man with a two-by-four in his eye who points out a speck in a friend's eye?

Can you honestly imagine a somber Jesus bouncing children on his knee?

No, I think Jesus smiled. I think he smiled a bit *at* people and a lot *with* people. I think he was the type of guy that people wanted to be near. I think he was the type of guy who was always invited to the party.

Consider, for example, the wedding at Cana. We often talk about this wedding as the place where Jesus turned the water into wine. But why did Jesus go to the wedding in the first place? The answer is found in the second verse of John 2: "Jesus and his followers were also invited to the wedding" (NCV).

When the bride and groom were putting the guest list together, Jesus' name was included. And when Jesus showed up with a half dozen friends, the invitation wasn't rescinded. Whoever was hosting this party was happy to have Jesus present.

"Be sure to put Jesus' name on the list," he might have said. "He really lightens up a party."

Jesus wasn't invited because he was a celebrity. He wasn't one yet. The invitation wasn't motivated by his miracles. He'd yet to perform any. Why did they invite him?

I suppose they liked him. Big deal? I think so. I think it's significant that common folk in a little town enjoyed being with Jesus. I think it's noteworthy that the Almighty didn't act high and mighty. The Holy One wasn't holier-than-thou. The one who knew it all wasn't a know-it-all. The one who made the stars didn't keep his head in them. The one who owns all the stuff on earth never strutted it.

Never. He could have. Oh, how he could have!

He could have been a name-dropper: *Did I ever tell you about the time Moses and I went up on the mountain?*

He could have been a show-off: *Hey, want me to beam you into the twentieth century?*

He could have been a smart aleck: *I know what you're thinking. Want me to prove it?*

He could have been highbrow and uppity: *I've got some property on Jupiter . . .*

Jesus could have been all of these, but he wasn't.

His purpose was not to show off but to show up. He

went to great pains to be as human as the guy down the street. He didn't need to study, but he still went to the synagogue. He had no need for income, but he still worked in the workshop. He had known the fellowship of angels and had heard the harps of heaven, yet he still went to parties thrown by tax collectors. And upon his shoulders rested the challenge of redeeming creation, but he still took time to walk for miles to go to a wedding in Cana.

As a result, people liked him. Oh, there were those who chafed at his claims. They called him a blasphemer, but they never called him a braggart. They accused him of heresy but never arrogance. He was branded as a radical but never called unapproachable.

There is no hint that he ever used his heavenly status for personal gain. Ever. You don't get the impression that his neighbors grew sick of his haughtiness and asked, "Well, who do you think made you God?"

His faith made him likable, not detestable. Jesus was accused of much, but of being a grump, sourpuss, or self-centered jerk? No. People didn't groan when he appeared. They didn't duck for cover when he entered the room.

He called them by name.

He listened to their stories.

He answered their questions.

He visited their sick relatives and helped their sick friends.

He fished with fishermen and ate lunch with the little guy and spoke words of resounding affirmation. He went to enough parties that he was criticized for hanging out with rowdy people and questionable crowds.

People were drawn to Jesus. He was always on the guest list. Thousands came to hear him. Hundreds chose to follow him. They shut down their businesses and walked away from careers to be with him. His purpose statement read: "I came to give life with joy and abundance" (John 10:10 THE VOICE). Jesus was happy and wants us to be the same.

Jesus' mission statement

When the angels announced the arrival of the Messiah, they proclaimed "good news of a great joy" (Luke 2:10 RSV), not "bad news of a great duty."

Would people say the same of us? Where did we get the notion that a good Christian is a solemn Christian? Who started the rumor that the sign of a disciple is a long face? How did we create this idea that the truly gifted are the heavyhearted?

May I state an opinion that could raise an eyebrow? May I tell you why I think Jesus went to that wedding in Cana? I think he went to the wedding to—now hold on, hear me out—I think Jesus went to the wedding to have fun.

Think about it. It had been a tough season. This wedding occurred after he had just spent forty days in the desert. No food or water. A standoff with the devil. A week breaking in some greenhorn Galileans. A job change. He had left home. It hadn't been easy. A break would be welcome. A good meal with some good wine and some good friends . . . Well, it sounded pretty nice.

So off they went.

His purpose wasn't to turn the water into wine. That was a favor for his friends.

His purpose wasn't to show his power. The wedding host didn't even know what Jesus did.

His purpose wasn't to preach. There is no record of a sermon.

This leaves only one reason. Fun. *Yay!* Jesus went to the wedding because he liked the people, he liked the food, and, heaven forbid, he may have even wanted to swirl the bride around the dance floor a time or two. (After all, he's planning a big wedding himself. Maybe he wanted the practice?)

Jesus was a likable fellow. And his disciples should *us, me!* be the same. I'm not talking debauchery, drunkenness, and adultery. I'm not endorsing compromise, coarseness, or obscenity. I am simply crusading for the freedom to enjoy a good joke, enliven a dull party, and appreciate a fun evening.

Maybe these thoughts catch you by surprise. They do me. It's been a while since I pegged Jesus as a party lover. But he was. His foes accused him of eating too much, drinking too much, and hanging out with the wrong people! I must confess: it's been a while since I've been accused of having too much fun. How about you?

What sort of portrait of Jesus hangs on the walls of your mind? Is he sad, somber, angry? Are his lips pursed? Is he judging you? If so, visualize the laughing Christ on my wall. I've needed the reminder more times than I can say. Jesus laughed. He had fun. He was always invited to the party, because people wanted to be near him. They didn't fear his judgment. They knew he wouldn't try to shut things down.

Who could be relied on to be the life of the party *Jesus at the wedding* more than the one who came to give life with joy and abundance?

Scripture references: John 2:1–11; Matthew 11:19

Chapter 9

Was everyone invited to sit at Jesus' table?

Writings from He Gets Us

We were looking at the life of Jesus to see who he really was, and we noticed something curious: he spent a lot of time around the dinner table. Many of his most frequently quoted messages and standout stories happened while sharing a meal with others. And those "others" around the table were a remarkably diverse cast. He shared meals with outcasts. He spent time with the self-righteous religious elite. He cared for people who had broken every rule and were seen as unclean. He dined at the tables of the wealthy men whose riches were won with lies and corruption. Some of those men gave up comfortable lifestyles to follow him. He crossed racial boundaries to the shock of many around him. He invited everyone to the table. When asked why he did so, he replied, "The reason I was born and came into the world is to testify to the truth. Everyone on the side of truth listens to me" (John 18:37).

It was radical at the time. No one was that inclusive. The religious do-gooders began to whisper behind his back. They called him a friend of sinners. It was supposed to be an insult, but Jesus wore it proudly. He was a friend to everyone. And what do friends do? They eat dinner together and share in each other's lives.

Strangers eating together and becoming friends. What a simple concept, and yet, we're pretty sure it would turn our own modern world upside down the same way Jesus turned his around two thousand years ago. That's really why we made this video in the first place. There are divisions and broken relationships everywhere. Judgmentalism and hypocrisy are on the rise. We see people who claim to be followers of Jesus taking his open invitation and turning it into an exclusive club.

The name of Jesus has been used by some to harm and divide, but if you look at how he lived, you see how backward that really is. Jesus was not exclusive. He was radically inclusive. What would our world look like if that were the norm? If strangers became friends over the dinner table as they did around Jesus?

Writings from Max Lucado

When you read Matthew's account of the Last Supper, one incredible truth surfaces. Jesus is the person behind it all. It is Jesus who selected the place, designated the time, and set the meal in order. "The chosen time is near. I will have the Passover with my followers at your house" (Matthew 26:18 NCV).

And at the supper, Jesus was not a guest but the host. " Jesus . . . gave *it* to the disciples." The subject of the verbs is the message of the event: "Jesus took . . . blessed . . . broke . . . gave. . ." (Matthew 26:26 NKJV).

And at the supper, Jesus is not the served but the

servant. It was Jesus who, during the supper, put on the garb of a servant and washed the disciples' feet (John 13:5).

Jesus was the most active one at the table. Jesus is not portrayed as the one who reclined and received but as the one who served and gave.

He still does. The Lord's Supper is a gift to you. The Lord's Supper is a sacrament,[4] not a sacrifice.[5]

Often we think of the supper as a performance, a time when we are on-stage and God is the audience. A ceremony in which we do the work and he does the watching. That's not how it was intended. If it was, Jesus would have taken his seat at the table and relaxed.[6]

That's not what he did. He, instead, fulfilled his role as a rabbi by guiding his disciples through the Passover. He fulfilled his role as a servant by washing their feet. And he fulfilled his role as a Savior by granting them forgiveness of sins.

He was in charge. He was on center stage. He was the person behind and in the moment.

And he still is.

It is the Lord's Table you sit at. It is the Lord's Supper you eat. Just as Jesus prayed for his disciples, Jesus begs God for us.[7] When you are called to the table, it might be an emissary who gives the letter, but it is Jesus who wrote it.

It is a holy invitation. A sacred sacrament bidding you to leave the chores of life and enter his splendor.

He meets you at the table.

And when the bread is broken, Christ breaks it. When the wine is poured, Christ pours it. And when your burdens are lifted, it is because the King in the apron has drawn near.

Think about that the next time you go to the table.

One last thought.

What happens on earth is just a warm-up for what will happen in heaven.[8] So the next time the Messenger calls you to the table, drop what you are doing and go. Be blessed and be fed and, most important, be sure you're still eating at his table when he calls us home.

Scripture references: Mark 2:13–17; Luke 19:1–10; Matthew 9:36–38; Luke 5:31–32

Chapter 10

Did Jesus struggle to be a good role model?

Writings from He Gets Us

Christians believe Jesus lived a perfect life. For others, that's hard to believe. Jesus set a high bar for himself and for others. He taught things such as: love your enemies, forgive those who've intentionally wronged you, and don't judge others. Easy in theory. Tougher in practice.

It must not have been easy for Jesus to practice what

he'd preached. When he was being mocked, surely, he was tempted to belittle his persecutors. When he was betrayed by a close friend, he could have berated him publicly. Ultimately, when he was being crucified, he didn't condemn his accusers or executioners. He forgave them.

When we realized how hard it must have been, even for Jesus, we recognized that he faced similar pressure to be a good example that we do today.

It's tough to always set the right example for our kids or friends or neighbors. Fortunately, there are many people trying hard and doing a great job at it. We tried to celebrate all those who are striving to pass the good on to others, to recognize the joy of being a positive role model, all the while acknowledging the challenge and struggle it is to always be on your best behavior.

Writings from Max Lucado

Aside from geography and chronology, our story is the same as the disciples'. We weren't in Jerusalem, and we weren't alive that night Jesus washed the feet of his followers. But what Jesus did for them, he is still doing. He is still cleansing hearts from sin.

John told us, "We are *being cleansed* from every sin by the blood of Jesus."[9] In other words, we are *always being cleansed*. The cleansing is not a promise for the future but a reality in the present. Let a speck of dust fall on the soul of a saint, and it is washed away. Let a spot of filth land on the heart of God's child, and the filth is wiped away. Jesus still cleans his disciples' feet. Jesus still washes away stains. Jesus still purifies his people.

Our Savior kneels down and gazes upon the darkest acts of our lives. But rather than recoil in horror, he reaches out in kindness and says, "I can clean that if you want." And from the basin of his grace, he scoops a palm full of mercy and washes away our sin.

But that's not all he does. Because he lives in us, you and I can do the same. Because he has forgiven us, we can forgive others. Because he has a forgiving heart, we can have a forgiving heart. We can have a heart like his.

"Now that I, your Lord and Teacher, have washed your feet, you also should wash one another's feet. I have set you an example that you should do as I have done for you" (John 13:14–15).

Jesus washes our feet for two reasons. The first is to give us mercy; the second is to give us a message, and that message is simply this: Jesus offers unconditional grace; we are to offer unconditional grace. The mercy of Christ preceded our mistakes; our mercy must precede the mistakes of others. Those in the circle of Christ had no doubt of his love; those in our circles should have no doubts about ours.

What does it mean to have a heart like his? It means to kneel as Jesus knelt, touching the grimy parts of the people we are stuck with and washing away their unkindnesses with kindness. Or as Paul wrote, "Be kind and loving to each other, and forgive each other just as God forgave you in Christ" (Ephesians 4:32 NCV).

The genius of Jesus' example is that the burden of bridge building falls on the strong one, not on the weak one. The one who is innocent is the one who makes the gesture.

And you know what happens? More often than not, if the one in the right volunteers to wash the feet of the one in the wrong, both parties get on their knees. Don't we all think we are right? Hence we wash each other's feet.

Please understand. *Relationships don't thrive because the guilty are punished but because the forgiven are merciful.*

Yes, Jesus felt the pressure to be a good role model. We know this because he was human too. He can relate to the pressures that we put on ourselves and that society places on our shoulders. He gets us.

Scripture references: John 13:12–17; Matthew 5:38–40; Luke 22:47–53

Part 4

Activism & Justice

Chapter 11

How did Jesus deal with injustice?

Writings from He Gets Us

No matter what we think of Christianity, most people can agree that Jesus set a pretty good example of peace and love. And it's not like he had an easy life.

He faced insurmountable controversy. So often he was the target of unjustified hate. How did he stifle his outrage?

Sometimes, he didn't. Jesus channeled his anger in defense of others when it really mattered. When he saw opportunists taking advantage of the poor, he confronted them without hesitation. But he knew how to pick his battles. Once, a group of men spit in Jesus' face, struck him, and slapped him, and yet, he did nothing to retaliate.

Living today, it's hard to imagine how he swallowed his rage. We've all noticed our blood boiling when politics come up in conversation, and we've felt the temptation to lash out on social media. It seems that every day, we're faced with something new to fight about. Even though our anger may be justified, it's taken a toll on our ability to engage with one another. And honestly, it doesn't feel good.

By telling this story, we reminded ourselves that even when we're tested and trolled, we have the option of rising above.

Writings from Max Lucado

"Get up, we must go. Look, here comes the man who has turned against me."[10]

The words were spoken about Judas. But they could

have been spoken about anyone. They could have been spoken about John, Peter, or James. They could have been spoken about Thomas, Andrew, or Nathanael. They could have been spoken about the Roman soldiers, to the Jewish leaders. They could have been spoken about Pilate, Herod, or Caiaphas. They could have been spoken to every person who abandoned him.

Judas did turn against him. What was your motive, Judas? Why did you do it? Were you trying to call his hand? Did you want the money? Were you seeking some attention?

The people did too. The crowd turned on Jesus. We wonder who was in the crowd. Who were the bystanders? Matthew just said they were people. Regular folks like you and me with bills to pay and kids to raise and jobs to do. Individually they never would have turned on Jesus, but collectively they wanted to kill him. Even the instantaneous healing of an amputated ear didn't sway them (Luke 22:51). They suffered from mob blindness. They blocked each other's vision of Jesus.

When the choice came between saving their skin and saving their friend, they chose to run. Oh, they stood for a while. Peter even pulled out his sword, went for the neck, and got an earlobe. But their courage was as fleeting as their feet. When they saw Jesus was going down, they got out.

The religious leaders did. Not surprising. Disappointing, though. They were the spiritual leaders of the nation. Men entrusted with the dispensing of goodness. Role models for the children. The pastors and Bible teachers of the community. "The leading priests and the whole Jewish council tried to find something false against Jesus so they could kill him."[11] Paint that passage black with injustice. Paint the arrest green with jealousy. Paint that scene red with innocent blood.

And paint Peter in a corner. For that's where he was. No place to go. Caught in his own mistake. Peter did exactly what he had said he wouldn't do. He had promised fervently only hours before, "Everyone else may stumble in their faith because of you, but I will not."[12] I hope Peter was hungry, because he ate those words.

Everyone turned against Jesus.

Though the kiss was planted by Judas, the betrayal was committed by all. Every person took a step, but no one took a stand. As Jesus left the garden, he walked alone. The world had turned against him.

Betray. The word is an eighth of an inch above *betroth* in the dictionary, but a world from *betroth* in life. It's a weapon found only in the hands of one you love. Your enemy has no such tool, for only a friend can betray. Betrayal is mutiny. It's a violation of a trust, an inside job.

Would that it were a stranger. Would that it were a random attack. Would that you were a victim of circumstances. But you aren't. You are a victim of a friend.

A sandpaper kiss is placed on your cheek. A promise is made with fingers crossed. You look to your friends, and your friends don't look back. You look to the system for justice. The system looks at you as a scapegoat.

You are betrayed. Bitten with a snake's kiss. It's more than rejection. Rejection opens a wound; betrayal pours the salt. It's more than loneliness. Loneliness leaves you in the cold; betrayal closes the door. It's more than mockery. Mockery plunges the knife; betrayal twists it. It's more than an insult. An insult attacks your pride; betrayal breaks your heart.

As I search for betrayal's synonyms, I keep seeing betrayal's victims. That unsigned letter in yesterday's mail that said, "My husband just told me he had an affair two years ago. I feel so alone." The phone call at home from the elderly woman whose drug-addicted son had taken her money. My friend in the Midwest who moved his family to take the promised job that never materialized. The single mother whose ex-husband brings his new girlfriend to her house when he comes to get the kids for the weekend. The seven-year-old girl infected with HIV. "I'm mad at my mother" were her words.

Betrayal . . . when your world turns against you.

Betrayal . . . where there is opportunity for love, there is opportunity for hurt.

When betrayal comes, what do you do? Get out? Get angry? Get even? You have to deal with it some way. Let's see how Jesus dealt with it.

Begin by noticing how Jesus saw Judas. "Jesus answered, 'Friend, do what you came to do.'"[13]

Of all the names I would have chosen for Judas, it would not have been "friend." What Judas did to Jesus was grossly unfair. There is no indication that Jesus ever mistreated Judas. There is no clue that Judas was ever left out or neglected. When, during the Last Supper, Jesus told the disciples that his betrayer sat at the table, they didn't turn to one another and whisper, "It's Judas. Jesus told us he would do this."

They didn't whisper it because Jesus never said it. He had known it. He had known what Judas would do, but he treated the betrayer as if he were faithful.

It's even more unfair when you consider the betrayal was Judas's idea. The religious leaders didn't seek him; Judas sought them. "What will you pay me for giving Jesus to you?" he asked.[14] The betrayal would have been more palatable had Judas been propositioned by the leaders, but he wasn't. He propositioned them.

And Judas's method . . . Again, why did it have to be a kiss?[15] And why did he have to call him "Teacher"? That's a title of respect. The incongruity of his words, deeds, and actions—I wouldn't have called Judas "friend." But that is exactly what Jesus called him. Why? Jesus could see something we can't. Let me explain.

There was once a person in our world who brought my wife and me a lot of stress. She would call in the middle of the night. She was demanding and ruthless. She screamed at us in public. When she wanted something, she wanted it immediately, and she wanted it exclusively from us. But we never asked her to leave us alone. We never told her to bug someone else. We never tried to get even. After all, she was only a few months old.

It was easy for us to forgive our infant daughter's behavior because we knew she didn't know better.

Now, there is a world of difference between an innocent child and a deliberate Judas. But there is still a point to my story, and it is this: the way to handle a person's behavior is to understand the cause of it.

Jesus knew Judas had been seduced by a powerful foe. He was aware of the wiles of Satan's whispers (he had just heard them himself). He knew how hard it was for Judas to do what was right. He didn't justify what Judas did. He didn't minimize the deed. Nor did he release Judas from his choice. But he did look eye to eye with his betrayer and try to understand.

Perhaps you don't like that idea. Perhaps the thought of forgiveness is unrealistic. Perhaps the idea of trying to understand the Judases in our world is simply too gracious.

My response to you, then, is a question. What do you suggest? Will harboring the anger solve the problem? Will getting even, remove the hurt? Does hatred do any good?

Again, I'm not minimizing your hurt or justifying their actions. But I am saying that justice won't come this side of eternity. And demanding that your enemy get his or her share of pain will, in the process, be most painful to you.

May I gently but firmly remind you of something you know but may have forgotten? Life is not fair.

That's not pessimism; it's fact. That's not a complaint; it's just the way things are. I don't like it. Neither do you. We want life to be fair. Ever since the kid down the block got a bike and we didn't, we've been saying the same thing, "That's not fair." But at some point someone needs to say to us, "Who ever told you life was going to be fair?" God didn't. He didn't say, "*If* you have many kinds of troubles . . ." He said, "*When* you have many kinds of troubles . . ."[16]

Troubles are part of the package. Betrayals are part of our troubles. Don't be surprised when betrayals come. Don't look for fairness here—look instead where Jesus looked.

Jesus looked to the future. Read his words: "In the future you will see the Son of Man . . . coming" (Matthew 26:64 NCV).

While surrounded by enemies, he kept his mind on his Father. While abandoned on earth, he kept his heart on home. "In the future you will see the Son of Man sitting at the right hand of God, the Powerful One, and coming on clouds in the sky."[17]

"My kingdom does not belong to this world," Jesus told Pilate. "My kingdom is from another place."[18]

Jesus took a long look into the homeland. Long

enough to count his friends. "I could ask my Father, and he would give me . . . twelve armies of angels."[19] And seeing them up there gave him strength down here.

By the way, his friends are your friends. The Father's loyalty to Jesus is the Father's loyalty to you. When you feel betrayed, remember that. When you see the torches and feel the betrayer's kiss, remember the Father's words: "I will never leave you; I will never abandon you."[20]

Scripture references: Matthew 5:38–48;
Luke 22:47–53; Mark 12:13–17

Chapter 12

How would Jesus be judged today?

Writings from He Gets Us

We were musing about how Jesus and his disciples were viewed in his day. If the authorities or religious leaders saw them walking down the street or hanging out on the corner, what would they have thought of them? It suddenly hit us. They would've been seen as trouble-makers. And Jesus was their ringleader. Matthew, one of his followers, was a Jew who formerly collected taxes for the Romans. In essence, he was seen as a lowlife traitor.

Some disciples violently opposed Herod, the king. Others were seen as uneducated dropouts. They were labeled and called many harsh things. But more important, they were seen as a threat to the establishment, which meant the people in power and the upper classes didn't want them in their neighborhoods or synagogues.

It's no different today. If we see youths of a different race or culture dressed a certain way or wearing their hair differently, we often make immediate judgments about them. Usually negative ones. It might make us uncomfortable or even unfriendly toward them. It's an unconscious bias we all have toward people who are different from us. We don't know the individual, yet we've already labeled them.

Jesus didn't judge others by their looks. He looked at their hearts. That meant reaching out to people who were outside his circle or society's mainstream to get to know them individually. He was criticized, even mocked, for doing so, but he didn't care because he loved all, even if it meant he would be wrongly judged for the friends he made and the company he kept.

Something interesting happened while we were producing this video. We wanted to use people we thought would immediately elicit judgment from others. You'll see that nobody is doing anything wrong or illegal. Maybe they're running down an alley, skateboarding, hanging out on a corner, or hopping a fence, but viewers have been conditioned by society to make assumptions that they're up to no good. Probably doing something illegal or criminal.

It was very intentional to point out the unconscious biases people have and that we need to overcome if we're going to build trust, love, and peace with each other.

Writings from Max Lucado

Suppose your past sins were made public? Suppose you were to stand on a stage while a film of every secret and selfish second was projected on the screen behind you?

Would you not crawl beneath the rug? Would you not scream for the heavens to have mercy? And would you not feel just a fraction of what Christ felt on the cross? The icy displeasure of a sin-hating God?

Christ carried all our sins in his body (1 Peter 2:24).

See Christ on the cross? That's a gossiper hanging there. See Jesus? Embezzler. Liar. Bigot. See the crucified carpenter? He's a wife beater. Porn addict and murderer. See Bethlehem's boy? Call him by his other names— Adolf Hitler, Osama bin Laden, and Jeffrey Dahmer.

You're probably thinking, *Hold on. Don't lump Christ with those evildoers. Don't place his name in the same sentence with theirs!*

I didn't. *He* did. Indeed, he did more. More than place his name in the same sentence, he placed himself in their place. And yours. With hands nailed open he invited God, "Treat me as you would treat them!" And God did. In an act that broke the heart of the Father, yet honored the holiness of heaven, sin-purging judgment flowed over the sinless Son of the ages. Everything the story had been building to landed at this moment with one final phrase.

Stop and listen. Can you imagine the final cry from the cross? The sky is dark. The other two victims are moaning. The jeering mouths are silent. Perhaps there is thunder. Perhaps there is weeping. Perhaps there is silence. Then Jesus draws a deep breath, pushes his feet down on that Roman nail, and cries, "It is finished!" (John 19:30 NKJV).

Jesus didn't quit. But don't think for one minute that he wasn't tempted to. Watch him wince as he hears his apostles backbite and quarrel. Look at him weep as he sits at Lazarus's tomb, or hear him wail as he claws the ground of Gethsemane.

Did he ever want to quit? You bet.

That's why his words are so splendid.

"It is finished!"

The history-long plan of redeeming humanity was finished. The message of God to humans was finished. The works done by Jesus as a man on earth were finished. The task of selecting and training ambassadors was finished. The job was finished. The song had been sung. The blood had been poured. The sacrifice had been made. The sting of death had been removed. It was over. A cry of defeat? Hardly. Had his hands not been fastened down, I dare say that a triumphant fist would have punched the dark sky. No, this was not a cry of despair. It was a cry of completion. A cry of victory. A cry of fulfillment. Yes, even a cry of relief.

The fighter remained. And thank God that he did. Thank God that he endured, because you cannot deal with your own sins. "Only God can forgive sins" (Mark 2:7 NCV). Jesus is "the Lamb of God, who takes away the sin of the world!" (John 1:29 NCV).

How did God deal with your debt?

Did he overlook it? He could have. He could have

burned the statement. He could have ignored your bounced checks. But would a holy God do that? *Could* a holy God do that? No. He wouldn't be holy. Besides, is that how we want God to run his world—ignoring our sin and thereby endorsing our rebellion?

Did he punish you for your sins? Again, he could have. He could have crossed out your name in the Book of Life and wiped you off the face of the earth. But would a loving God do that? *Could* a loving God do that? He loves his children with an everlasting love. Experiencing no condemnation in Christ (Romans 8:1) means no separation, either (Romans 8:38–39).

So what did he do? "God put the world square with himself through the Messiah, giving the world a fresh start by offering forgiveness of sins. . . . How? you ask. In Christ. God put the wrong on him who never did anything wrong, so we could be put right with God" (2 Corinthians 5:19, 21 THE MESSAGE).

The cross included a "putting on." God put our wrongs on Christ so he could put Christ's righteousness on us.

Scripture references: Matthew 11:19;
Luke 5:29-32; Luke 6:6-11

Chapter 13

Did Jesus face criticism?

Writings from He Gets Us

We live in an era of social trends and influencers who mold the culture around us. Considerations about the impact of influencer voices, greased the cogs in our minds and shifted our attention to one of the most famous influencers to ever live.

Jesus had a following, to say the least. People came to him from every quarter to hear about his extreme views on love. This is no different from the thousands of subscribers or followers that influencers boast on today's social platforms, and just like those influencers, his message was not without its detractors. They wanted him canceled.

Studies indicate that 64 percent of respondents believe that cancel culture is a direct threat to their freedom. For Jesus, cancel culture did not put his freedom at risk. It put his life at risk. However, such threats did not deter him from delivering his radical truth. This willingness to take a stand is a conviction we wanted to permeate into the visuals for this topic. We selected imagery that reflects the strain of standing up for your beliefs even when the masses aim to vanquish your voice; a feeling that Jesus knew all too well.

Writings from Max Lucado

We who follow Christ do so for the reason that he's been there . . .

He's been to Bethlehem, wearing barn rags and hearing sheep crunch. Suckling milk and shivering against the cold. All divinity content to cocoon itself in an eight-pound body and to sleep on a cow's supper. Millions who face the chill of empty pockets or the fears of sudden change turn to Christ. Why?

Because he's been there.

He's been to Nazareth, where he made deadlines and paid bills; to Galilee, where he recruited direct reports and separated fighters; to Jerusalem, where he stared down critics and stood up against cynics.

We have our Nazareths as well—demands and due dates. Jesus wasn't the last to build a team; accusers didn't disappear with Jerusalem's temple. Why seek Jesus' help with your challenges? Because he's been there. To Nazareth, to Galilee, to Jerusalem.

But most of all, he's been to the grave. Not as a visitor but as a corpse. Buried amid the cadavers. Numbered among the dead. Heart silent and lungs vacant. Body wrapped and grave sealed. The cemetery. He's been buried there.

You haven't yet. But you will be. And since you will, don't you need someone who knows the way out?

"[God] has given us new birth into a living hope through the resurrection of Jesus Christ from the dead"; "He destroyed death, and through the Good News he showed us the way to have life that cannot be destroyed" (1 Peter 1:3; 2 Timothy 1:10 NCV).

Jesus was constantly criticized by others, but he never criticized in return. He didn't get angry or discouraged because of what the Pharisees, scribes, or nonbelievers said about him. Jesus did what we're taught as children to do—*treat others the way you want to be treated*. Negative criticism is a distraction from God's purpose for your life.

Scripture references: Matthew 23:1–34; Luke 11:37–52

Chapter 14

Was Jesus fed up with politics?

<u>Writings from He Gets Us</u>

In Jesus' time, communities were deeply divided by bitter differences in religious beliefs, political positions, income inequality, legal status, and ethnic differences. Sound familiar?

Jesus lived in the middle of a culture war too. And though the political systems were different (not exactly a representative democracy), the greed, hypocrisy, and oppression different groups used to get their way were very similar.

Let's set the scene.

Jesus was born at the height of the Roman Empire's power. They'd conquered most of the known world, and Israel was no exception. Unlike previous empires that would try to destroy cultures by displacing conquered peoples' leaders, the Romans didn't force people to change their religion or customs as long as they kept their obligations to the empire. Rome would install a client king (a puppet government) and exact tribute (cash) in lots of different ways. Families were charged taxes per person— farmers on crops, fishermen on catches, and travelers were charged fees to use the roads. This was in addition to local business and religious taxes charged by priests.

In Israel, political and religious factions were one and the same. Back then, it was Pharisees and Sadducees. Today, we have conservatives and liberals.

The Pharisees were the most religiously conservative leaders. They had the most influence among the common working poor, who were the majority. They believed that a king would come one day to conquer Rome with violence and free their nation. Some preyed upon a mostly illiterate population by adding extra rules and requirements that were designed to force the working poor into a posture of subjugation.

The Sadducees were wealthy aristocrats who had a vested financial interest in Roman rule. They were in charge of the temple, and they didn't believe any savior king was coming. They made themselves wealthy by exacting unfair taxes and fees from the labor of their own people and by contriving moneymaking schemes that forced the poor to pay exorbitant prices to participate in temple sacrifice—a critical part of their religion.

There were zealot groups who hid in the hills and violently resisted Roman occupation, and then there were the Samaritans, often oppressed and marginalized because of their racial and ethnic identities.

And so, the common farmer, fisherman, or craftsman's family lived through a highly volatile political period. Overbearing religious leaders who despised and oppressed them, wealthy elites who ripped them off, racial and ethnic tension with neighbors, and sporadic violent outbreaks between an oppressive occupying army.

So where was Jesus in all of this? Did he align with the religious elites? With the wealthy and powerful? Or did he start an uprising to overthrow them?

None of the above.

He went from town to town, offering hope, new life, and modeling a different way to live and to change the world. Instead of pursuing power, money, or religious authority, he shared a loving and sacrificially generous way of living. He chose not to go along with the schemes others used to impact the world. Instead, he championed a better way.

And so, each of these political groups saw him as a threat. The Pharisees recognized his movement as an affront to their authority—exposing the hypocrisy of their practices. The Sadducees saw Jesus as a threat to their power and wealth because he exposed their moneymaking schemes. The Zealots violently rejected one of the essential themes of Jesus' movement: love your enemy.

In the end, it took all three of these groups to have him killed. A Zealot (Judas) betrayed Jesus' location to those seeking to arrest him, the Sadducees brought him before the Romans to be executed, and when the Romans couldn't find a crime committed, the Pharisees rallied the people to force Rome's hand.

Isn't it funny how political foes can come together to destroy a common enemy that threatens their designs? But in spite of their best efforts, his execution was only the beginning of a movement that continues to impact the world thousands of years later. Jesus' movement was so impactful because he actively resisted and rejected participating in culture-war politics.

Writings from Max Lucado

There's no doubt that we have heard political ads ad nauseam. Republicans attempting to stay "on message." Democrats resolving to swing the party back "on message." The phrase carries the idea of the central theme, the big points, the idea we exist to promote.

Avoid rabbit trails. Anchor to core values. Relentlessly promote unique ideas. Stay on message.

I've asked myself, how are Christians doing when it comes to staying on message? That question begs a prior one. What is our message? Most search results would say the Christian message is "pro-life, traditional marriage; more red than blue, more conservative than liberal."

But is this our core message? Paddle upstream to the earliest framers of the Christian message. The story the first disciples were dying to tell was this: the grace of Jesus Christ.

"Though we were spiritually dead because of the things we did against God, he gave us new life with Christ. You have been saved by God's grace. . . . You have been saved by grace through believing. You did not save yourselves; it was a gift from God. . . . In Christ Jesus, God made us to do good works, which God planned in advance for us to live our lives doing" (Ephesians 2:5, 8, 10 NCV).

Behold the fruit of grace: raised by God, saved by God, seated with God. Gifted, equipped, and commissioned. *Grace* is the word God uses to describe his radical commitment to redeem and restore to himself a people with whom he will reign forever. Grace changes everything! We are spiritually alive. Heavenly positioned. Connected to God. A billboard of mercy. An honored child. This is the "aggressive forgiveness we call *grace*" (Romans 5:20 THE MESSAGE).

Grace declares that God knew what he was doing when he made you and is dead serious about saving you for something out of this world. Grace goes where no government can. Grace speaks to the core questions: Why are we here? Where are we headed? Does anyone care? Grace gets to the bottom of this thing called life.

Grace. This is the big message of the Christian hope,

the unique idea we bring to the social conversation. Let's major in this story. Let's unleash our clearest thoughts on this question: How can we best articulate the greatest announcement in history? "From his fullness we have all received, grace upon grace" (John 1:16 ESV).

Let's hold to deep-seated convictions about family and the practice of faith. But let's begin and end with the highest of all hopes: "The grace of God has appeared, bringing salvation to all people" (Titus 2:11 NASB). The message of Christianity from Jesus himself is that we know everyone is broken by sin, but God's grace—his granting to us what we don't actually deserve—changes us and calls us to share his love with others who are broken like us.

Scripture references: Matthew 9:35–38; Luke 19:10

Scripture
Reference Guide

PART 1: REAL LIFE

1. Was Jesus ever stressed?

> You see, at just the right time, when we were
> still powerless, Christ died for the ungodly.
> Very rarely will anyone die for a righteous per-
> son, though for a good person someone might
> possibly dare to die. But God demonstrates his
> own love for us in this: While we were still sin-
> ners, Christ died for us.
>
> **Romans 5:6–8 NIV**

2. What would Jesus think of teen moms?

Now the birth of Jesus Christ was as follows: After His mother Mary was betrothed to Joseph, before they came together, she was found with child of the Holy Spirit. Then Joseph her husband, being a just man, and not wanting to make her a public example, was minded to put her away secretly. But while he thought about these things, behold, an angel of the Lord appeared to him in a dream, saying, "Joseph, son of David, do not be afraid to take to you Mary your wife, for that which is conceived in her is of the Holy Spirit. And she will bring forth a Son, and you shall call His name Jesus, for He will save His people from their sins."

So all this was done that it might be fulfilled which was spoken by the Lord through the prophet, saying: "Behold, the virgin shall be with child, and bear a Son, and they shall call His name Immanuel," which is translated, "God with us."

Then Joseph, being aroused from sleep, did as the angel of the Lord commanded him and took to him his wife, and did not know her till she had brought forth her firstborn Son. And he called His name Jesus.

Matthew 1:18–25 NKJV

And she gave birth to her first son. Because there were no rooms left in the inn, she wrapped the baby with pieces of cloth and laid him in a feeding trough.

Luke 2:7 NCV

3. Was Jesus ever lonely?

On hearing it, many of his disciples said, "This is a hard teaching. Who can accept it?"

Aware that his disciples were grumbling about this, Jesus said to them, "Does this offend you? Then what if you see the Son of Man ascend to where he was before! The Spirit gives life; the flesh counts for nothing. The words I have spoken to you—they are full of the Spirit and life. Yet there are some of you who do not believe." For Jesus had known from the beginning which of them did not believe and who would betray him. He went on to say, "This is why I told you that no one can come to me unless the Father has enabled them."

From this time many of his disciples turned back and no longer followed him.

"You do not want to leave too, do you?" Jesus asked the Twelve.

Simon Peter answered him, "Lord, to whom shall we go? You have the words of eternal life. We have come to believe and to know that you are the Holy One of God."

Then Jesus replied, "Have I not chosen you, the Twelve? Yet one of you is a devil!" (He meant Judas, the son of Simon Iscariot, who, though one of the Twelve, was later to betray him.)

John 6:60–71, NIV

Peter Denies Jesus, and Weeps Bitterly

Now Peter sat outside in the courtyard. And a servant girl came to him, saying, "You also were with Jesus of Galilee."

But he denied it before them all, saying, "I do not know what you are saying."

And when he had gone out to the gateway, another girl saw him and said to those who were there, "This fellow also was with Jesus of Nazareth."

But again he denied with an oath, "I do not know the Man!"

And a little later those who stood by came up and said to Peter, "Surely you also are one of them, for your speech betrays you."

Then he began to curse and swear, saying, "I do not know the Man!"

Immediately a rooster crowed. And Peter remembered the word of Jesus who had said to him, "Before the rooster crows, you will deny Me three times." So he went out and wept bitterly.

Matthew 26:69–75 NKJV

4. Can I judge without being judgmental?

"Don't judge others, or you will be judged."

Matthew 7:1 NCV

"Do not judge, and you will not be judged. Do not condemn, and you will not be condemned. Forgive, and you will be forgiven."

Luke 6:37 NIV

"Do not judge according to appearance, but judge with righteous judgment."

John 7:24 NKJV

PART 2: STRUGGLE

<u>5. Did Jesus live in poverty?</u>

Jesus said to him, "The foxes have holes to live in, and the birds have nests, but the Son of Man has no place to rest his head."

Matthew 8:20 NCV

Jesus said, "Don't let your hearts be troubled. Trust in God, and trust in me. There are many rooms in my Father's house; I would not tell you this if it were not true. I am going there to prepare a place for you. After I go and prepare a place for you, I will come back and take you to be with me so that you may be where I am."

John 14: 1–3 NCV

<u>6. Why did Jesus cry?</u>

Then, when Mary came where Jesus was, and saw Him, she fell down at His feet, saying to Him, "Lord, if You had been here, my brother would not have died."

Therefore, when Jesus saw her weeping,

and the Jews who came with her weeping, He groaned in the spirit and was troubled. And He said, "Where have you laid him?"

They said to Him, "Lord, come and see."

Jesus wept. Then the Jews said, "See how He loved him!"

And some of them said, "Could not this Man, who opened the eyes of the blind, also have kept this man from dying?"

John 11:32–37 NKJV

7. Did Jesus ever mourn?

On Herod's birthday the daughter of Herodias danced for the guests and pleased Herod so much that he promised with an oath to give her whatever she asked. Prompted by her mother, she said, "Give me here on a platter the head of John the Baptist." The king was distressed, but because of his oaths and his dinner guests, he ordered that her request be granted and had John beheaded in the prison. His head was brought in on a platter and given to the girl, who carried it to her mother. John's disciples came and took his body and buried it. Then they went and told Jesus.

When Jesus heard what had happened, he withdrew by boat privately to a solitary place. Hearing of this, the crowds followed him on foot from the towns. When Jesus landed and saw a large crowd, he had compassion on them and healed their sick.

Matthew 14:6–14 NIV

On his arrival, Jesus found that Lazarus had already been in the tomb for four days. Now Bethany was less than two miles from Jerusalem, and many Jews had come to Martha and Mary to comfort them in the loss of their brother. When Martha heard that Jesus was coming, she went out to meet him, but Mary stayed at home.

"Lord," Martha said to Jesus, "if you had been here, my brother would not have died. But I know that even now God will give you whatever you ask."

Jesus said to her, "Your brother will rise again."

Martha answered, "I know he will rise again in the resurrection at the last day."

Jesus said to her, "I am the resurrection and the life. The one who believes in me will live, even though they die; and whoever lives by believing in me will never die. Do you believe this?"

"Yes, Lord," she replied, "I believe that you are the Messiah, the Son of God, who is to come into the world."

After she had said this, she went back and called her sister Mary aside. "The Teacher is here," she said, "and is asking for you." When Mary heard this, she got up quickly and went to him. Now Jesus had not yet entered the village, but was still at the place where Martha had met him. When the Jews who had been with Mary in the house, comforting her, noticed how quickly she got up and went out, they followed her, supposing she was going to the tomb to mourn there.

When Mary reached the place where Jesus was and saw him, she fell at his feet and said, "Lord, if you had been here, my brother would not have died."

When Jesus saw her weeping, and the Jews who had come along with her also weeping, he was deeply moved in spirit and troubled. "Where have you laid him?" he asked.

"Come and see, Lord," they replied.

Jesus wept.

Then the Jews said, "See how he loved him!"

But some of them said, "Could not he who opened the eyes of the blind man have kept this man from dying?"

Jesus, once more deeply moved, came to the tomb. It was a cave with a stone laid across the entrance. "Take away the stone," he said.

"But, Lord," said Martha, the sister of the dead man, "by this time there is a bad odor, for he has been there four days."

Then Jesus said, "Did I not tell you that if you believe, you will see the glory of God?"

So they took away the stone. Then Jesus looked up and said, "Father, I thank you that you have heard me. I knew that you always hear me, but I said this for the benefit of the people standing here, that they may believe that you sent me."

When he had said this, Jesus called in a loud voice, "Lazarus, come out!" The dead man came out, his hands and feet wrapped with strips of linen, and a cloth around his face.

Jesus said to them, "Take off the grave clothes and let him go."

John 11:17–44 NIV

The Prayer in the Garden

Then Jesus came with them to a place called Gethsemane, and said to the disciples, "Sit here while I go and pray over there." And He took with Him Peter and the two sons of Zebedee, and He began to be sorrowful and deeply distressed. Then He said to them, "My soul is exceedingly sorrowful, even to death. Stay here and watch with Me."

He went a little farther and fell on His face, and prayed, saying, "O My Father, if it is possible, let this cup pass from Me; nevertheless, not as I will, but as You will."

Then He came to the disciples and found them sleeping, and said to Peter, "What! Could you not watch with Me one hour? Watch and pray, lest you enter into temptation. The spirit indeed is willing, but the flesh is weak."

Again, a second time, He went away and prayed, saying, "O My Father, if this cup cannot pass away from Me unless I drink it, Your will be done." And He came and found them asleep again, for their eyes were heavy.

So He left them, went away again, and prayed the third time, saying the same words.

Then He came to His disciples and said to them, "Are you still sleeping and resting? Behold, the hour is at hand, and the Son of Man is being betrayed into the hands of sinners. Rise, let us be going. See, My betrayer is at hand."

Matthew 26:36–46 NKJV

PART 3: HOPE

8. Did Jesus have fun?

On the third day there was a wedding in Cana of Galilee, and the mother of Jesus was there. Now both Jesus and His disciples were invited to the wedding. And when they ran out of wine, the mother of Jesus said to Him, "They have no wine."

Jesus said to her, "Woman, what does your concern have to do with Me? My hour has not yet come."

His mother said to the servants, "Whatever He says to you, do it."

Now there were set there six waterpots of stone, according to the manner of purification of the Jews, containing twenty or thirty gallons apiece. Jesus said to them, "Fill the waterpots with water." And they filled them up to the brim. And He said to them, "Draw some out now, and take it to the master of the feast." And they took it. When the master of the feast had tasted the water that was made wine, and did not know where it came from (but the servants who had drawn the water knew), the master of the feast called the bridegroom. And he said to him, "Every man at the beginning sets out the good wine, and when the guests have well drunk, then the inferior. You have kept the good wine until now!"

This beginning of signs Jesus did in Cana of Galilee, and manifested His glory; and His disciples believed in Him.

John 2:1–11 NKJV

The Son of Man came, eating and drinking, and people say, "Look at him! He eats too much and drinks too much wine, and he is a friend of tax collectors and sinners." But wisdom is proved to be right by what she does.

Matthew 11:19 NCV

9. Was everyone invited to sit at Jesus' table?

Matthew the Tax Collector

Then He went out again by the sea; and all the multitude came to Him, and He taught them. As He passed by, He saw Levi the son of Alphaeus sitting at the tax office. And He said to him, "Follow Me." So he arose and followed Him.

Now it happened, as He was dining in Levi's house, that many tax collectors and sinners also sat together with Jesus and His disciples; for there were many, and they followed Him. And when the scribes and Pharisees saw Him eating with the tax collectors and sinners, they said to His disciples, "How is it that He eats and drinks with tax collectors and sinners?"

When Jesus heard it, He said to them, "Those who are well have no need of a physician, but those who are sick. I did not come to call the righteous, but sinners, to repentance."

Mark 2:13–17 NKJV

Zacchaeus the Tax Collector

Jesus entered Jericho and was passing through. A man was there by the name of Zacchaeus; he was a chief tax collector and was wealthy. He wanted to see who Jesus was, but because he was short he could not see over the crowd. So he ran ahead and climbed a sycamore-fig tree to see him, since Jesus was coming that way.

When Jesus reached the spot, he looked up and said to him, "Zacchaeus, come down immediately. I must stay at your house today." So he came down at once and welcomed him gladly.

All the people saw this and began to mutter, "He has gone to be the guest of a sinner."

But Zacchaeus stood up and said to the Lord, "Look, Lord! Here and now I give half of my possessions to the poor, and if I have cheated anybody out of anything, I will pay back four times the amount."

Jesus said to him, "Today salvation has come to this house, because this man, too, is a son of Abraham. For the Son of Man came to seek and to save the lost."

Luke 19:1–10 NIV

But when He saw the multitudes, He was moved with compassion for them, because they were weary and scattered, like sheep having no shepherd. Then He said to His disciples, "The harvest truly is plentiful, but the laborers are few. Therefore pray the Lord of the harvest to send out laborers into His harvest."

Matthew 9:36–38 NKJV

Jesus answered them, "It is not the healthy who need a doctor, but the sick. I have not come to invite good people but sinners to change their hearts and lives."

Luke 5:31–32 NCV

10. Did Jesus struggle to be a good role model?

So when He had washed their feet, taken His garments, and sat down again, He said to them, "Do you know what I have done to you? You call Me Teacher and Lord, and you say well, for so I am. If I then, your Lord and Teacher, have washed your feet, you also ought to wash one another's feet. For I have given you an example, that you should do as I have done to you. Most assuredly, I say to you, a servant is not greater than his master; nor is he who is sent greater than he who sent him.

If you know these things, blessed are you if you do them."

John 13:12–17 NKJV

"You have heard that it was said, 'Eye for eye, and tooth for tooth.' But I tell you, do not resist an evil person. If anyone slaps you on the right cheek, turn to them the other cheek also. And if anyone wants to sue you and take your shirt, hand over your coat as well."

Matthew 5:38–40 NIV

Betrayal and Arrest in Gethsemane

And while He was still speaking, behold, a multitude; and he who was called Judas, one of the twelve, went before them and drew near to Jesus to kiss Him. But Jesus said to him, "Judas, are you betraying the Son of Man with a kiss?"

When those around Him saw what was going to happen, they said to Him, "Lord, shall we strike with the sword?" And one of them struck the servant of the high priest and cut off his right ear.

But Jesus answered and said, "Permit even this." And He touched his ear and healed him.

Then Jesus said to the chief priests, captains of the temple, and the elders who had come to Him, "Have you come out, as against a robber, with swords and clubs? When I was with you daily in the temple, you did not try to seize Me. But this is your hour, and the power of darkness."

Luke 22:47–53 NKJV

PART 4: ACTIVISM & JUSTICE

11. How did Jesus deal with injustice?

Eye for Eye

You have heard that it was said, "Eye for eye, and tooth for tooth." But I tell you, do not resist an evil person. If anyone slaps you on the right cheek, turn to them the other cheek also. And if anyone wants to sue you and take your shirt, hand over your coat as well. If anyone forces you to go one mile, go with them two miles. Give to the one who asks you, and do not turn away from the one who wants to borrow from you."

Love for Enemies

"You have heard that it was said, 'Love your neighbor and hate your enemy.' But I tell you, love your enemies and pray for those who persecute you, that you may be children of your Father in heaven. He causes his sun to rise on the evil and the good, and sends rain on the righteous and the unrighteous. If you love those who love you, what reward will you get? Are not even the tax collectors doing that? And if you greet only your own people, what are you doing more than others? Do not even pagans do that? Be perfect, therefore, as your heavenly Father is perfect."

Matthew 5:38–48 NIV

Betrayal and Arrest in Gethsemane

While he was still speaking a crowd came up, and the man who was called Judas, one of the Twelve, was leading them. He approached Jesus to kiss him, but Jesus asked him, "Judas are you betraying the Son of Man with a kiss?

When Jesus' followers saw what was going to happen, they said, "Lord, should we strike with our swords?" And one of them struck the servant of the high priest, cutting off his right ear.

But Jesus answered, "No more of this!" And he touched the man's ear and healed him.

Then Jesus said to the chief priests, the officers of the temple guard, and the elders, who had come for him, "Am I leading a rebellion, that you have come with swords and clubs? Every day I was with you in the temple courts, and you did not lay a hand on me. But this is your hour—when darkness reigns."

Luke 22:47–53 NIV

Paying the Imperial Tax to Caesar

Later they sent some of the Pharisees and Herodians to Jesus to catch him in his words. They came to him and said, "Teacher, we know that you are a man of integrity. You aren't swayed by others, because you pay no attention to who they are; but you teach the way of God in accordance with the truth. Is it right to pay the imperial tax to Caesar or not? Should we pay or shouldn't we?"

But Jesus knew their hypocrisy. "Why are you trying to trap me?" he asked. "Bring me a denarius and let me look at it." They brought the coin, and he asked them, "Whose image is this? And whose inscription?"

"Caesar's," they replied.

Then Jesus said to them, "Give back to Caesar what is Caesar's and to God what is God's."

And they were amazed at him.

Mark 12:13–17 NIV

12. How would Jesus be judged today?

"The Son of Man came eating and drinking, and they say, 'Look, a glutton and a winebibber, a friend of tax collectors and sinners!' But wisdom is justified by her children."

Matthew 11:19 NKJV

Then Levi held a great banquet for Jesus at his house, and a large crowd of tax collectors and others were eating with them. But the Pharisees and the teachers of the law who belonged to their sect complained to his disciples, "Why do you eat and drink with tax collectors and sinners?"

Jesus answered them, "It is not the healthy

who need a doctor, but the sick. I have not come to call the righteous, but sinners to repentance."

Luke 5:29–32 NIV

Now it happened on another Sabbath, also, that He entered the synagogue and taught. And a man was there whose right hand was withered. So the scribes and Pharisees watched Him closely, whether He would heal on the Sabbath, that they might find an accusation against Him. But He knew their thoughts, and said to the man who had the withered hand, "Arise and stand here." And he arose and stood. Then Jesus said to them, "I will ask you one thing: Is it lawful on the Sabbath to do good or to do evil, to save life or to destroy?" And when He had looked around at them all, He said to the man, "Stretch out your hand." And he did so, and his hand was restored as whole as the other. But they were filled with rage, and discussed with one another what they might do to Jesus.

Luke 6:6–11 NKJV

13. Did Jesus face criticism?

A Warning Against Hypocrisy

Then Jesus said to the crowds and to his disciples: "The teachers of the law and the Pharisees sit in Moses' seat. So you must be careful to do everything they tell you. But do not do what they do, for they do not practice what they preach. They tie up heavy, cumbersome loads and put them on other people's shoulders, but they themselves are not willing to lift a finger to move them.

"Everything they do is done for people to see: They make their phylacteries wide and the tassels on their garments long; they love the place of honor at banquets and the most important seats in the synagogues; they love to be greeted with respect in the marketplaces and to be called 'Rabbi' by others.

"But you are not to be called 'Rabbi,' for you have one Teacher, and you are all brothers. And do not call anyone on earth 'father,' for you have one Father, and he is in heaven. Nor are you to be called instructors, for you have one Instructor, the Messiah. The greatest among you will be your servant. For those who exalt themselves will be humbled, and those who humble themselves will be exalted."

Seven Woes on the Teachers of the Law and the Pharisees

"Woe to you, teachers of the law and Pharisees, you hypocrites! You shut the door of the kingdom of heaven in people's faces. You yourselves do not enter, nor will you let those enter who are trying to.

"Woe to you, teachers of the law and Pharisees, you hypocrites! You travel over land and sea to win a single convert, and when you have succeeded, you make them twice as much a child of hell as you are.

"Woe to you, blind guides! You say, 'If anyone swears by the temple, it means nothing; but anyone who swears by the gold of the temple is bound by that oath.' You blind fools! Which is greater: the gold, or the temple that makes the gold sacred? You also say, 'If anyone swears by the altar, it means nothing; but anyone who swears by the gift on the altar is bound by that oath.' You blind men! Which is greater: the gift, or the altar that makes the gift sacred? Therefore, anyone who swears by the altar swears by it and by everything on it. And anyone who swears by the temple swears by it and by the one who dwells in it. And anyone who swears by heaven swears by God's throne and by the one who sits on it.

"Woe to you, teachers of the law and Pharisees, you hypocrites! You give a tenth of your spices—mint, dill and cumin. But you have neglected the more important matters of the law—justice, mercy and faithfulness. You should have practiced the latter, without neglecting the former. You blind guides! You strain out a gnat but swallow a camel.

"Woe to you, teachers of the law and Pharisees, you hypocrites! You clean the outside of the cup and dish, but inside they are full of greed and self-indulgence. Blind Pharisee! First clean the inside of the cup and dish, and then the outside also will be clean.

"Woe to you, teachers of the law and Pharisees, you hypocrites! You are like white-washed tombs, which look beautiful on the outside but on the inside are full of the bones of the dead and everything unclean. In the same way, on the outside you appear to people as righteous but on the inside you are full of hypocrisy and wickedness.

"Woe to you, teachers of the law and Pharisees, you hypocrites! You build tombs for the prophets and decorate the graves of the righteous. And you say, 'If we had lived in the days of our ancestors, we would not have taken part with them in shedding the blood of the prophets.' So you testify against yourselves that you are the descendants of those who murdered the prophets. Go ahead, then, and complete what your ancestors started!

"You snakes! You brood of vipers! How will you escape being condemned to hell? Therefore I am sending you prophets and sages and teachers. Some of them you will kill and crucify; others you will flog in your synagogues and pursue from town to town."

Matthew 23:1–34 NIV

Woe to the Pharisees and Lawyers

And as He spoke, a certain Pharisee asked Him to dine with him. So He went in and sat down to eat. When the Pharisee saw it, he marveled that He had not first washed before dinner.

Then the Lord said to him, "Now you Pharisees make the outside of the cup and dish clean, but your inward part is full of greed and wickedness. Foolish ones! Did not He who made the outside make the inside also? But rather give alms of such things as you have; then indeed all things are clean to you.

"But woe to you Pharisees! For you tithe mint and rue and all manner of herbs, and pass by justice and the love of God. These you ought to have done, without leaving the others undone. Woe to you Pharisees! For you love the best seats in the synagogues and greetings in the marketplaces. Woe to you, scribes and Pharisees, hypocrites! For you are like graves which are not seen, and the men who walk over them are not aware of them."

Then one of the lawyers answered and said to Him, "Teacher, by saying these things You reproach us also."

And He said, "Woe to you also, lawyers! For you load men with burdens hard to bear, and you yourselves do not touch the burdens with one of your fingers. Woe to you! For you build the tombs of the prophets, and your fathers killed them. In fact, you bear witness that you approve the deeds of your fathers; for they indeed killed them, and you build their tombs. Therefore the wisdom of God also said, 'I will send them prophets and apostles, and some of them they will kill and persecute,' that the blood of all the prophets which was shed from the foundation of the world may be required of this generation, from the blood of Abel to the blood of Zechariah who perished between the altar and the temple. Yes, I say to you, it shall be required of this generation.

"Woe to you lawyers! For you have taken away the key of knowledge. You did not enter in yourselves, and those who were entering in you hindered."

Luke 11:37–52 NKJV

14. Was Jesus fed up with politics?

The Workers Are Few

Jesus went through all the towns and villages, teaching in their synagogues, proclaiming the good news of the kingdom and healing every disease and sickness. When he saw the crowds, he had compassion on them, because they were harassed and helpless, like sheep without a shepherd. Then he said to his disciples, "The harvest is plentiful but the workers are few. Ask the Lord of the harvest, therefore, to send out workers into his harvest field."

Matthew 9:35–38 NIV

"The Son of Man came to find lost people and save them."

Luke 19:10 NCV

Notes

1. Taylor Clark, *Nerve: Poise Under Pressure, Serenity Under Stress, and the Brave New Science of Fear and Cool* (New York: Little, Brown, 2011), 100–101.
2. Clark, *Nerve*, 100–101.
3. Alan Mozes, "Traffic Jams Harm the Heart," HealthDay, March 13, 2009, https://consumer.healthday .com/cardiovascular-and-health-information-20/heart -attack-news-357/traffic-jams-harm-the-heart-624998 .html.
4. A sacrament is a gift from the Lord to his people.
5. A sacrifice is a gift of the people to the Lord.
6. There are sacrificial moments during the supper. We offer up prayers, confessions, and thanksgivings as sacrifice. But they are sacrifices of thanksgiving for a salvation received, not sacrifices of service for

a salvation desired. We don't say, "Look at what I've done." We instead, in awe, watch God and worship what he has done.

7. Romans 8:34.
8. Luke 12:37.
9. See Revelation 1:5.
10. Matthew 26:46 NCV, emphasis added.
11. Matthew 26:59 NCV.
12. Matthew 26:33 NCV.
13. Matthew 26:50 NCV.
14. Matthew 26:15 NCV.
15. Matthew 26:48–49.
16. James 1:2, NCV, emphasis added.
17. Matthew 26:64, NCV.
18. John 18:36, NCV.
19. Matthew 26:53, NCV.
20. Hebrews 13:5, NCV.

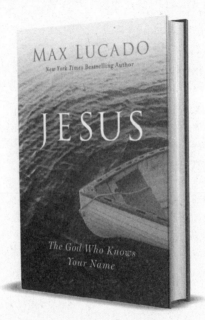

No Money Required
Pay with Love

Select one of each available item for your order.

Text for Prayer or Positivity

Got something going on in your life that could use some prayer or encouragement? Text 'Prayer' or 'Positivity' to the number below to have a volunteer pray for you or just send some words of encouragement.

(833) 201-3790

Read About Jesus

Want to read more about Jesus but don't know where to start? Try these easy reading plans.

Reading Plan 1

Reading Plan 2

Reading Plan 3

Connect

Get connected with someone near you who can help you learn more about Jesus and his life, or get plugged into a group where you can bring your questions about life and faith.

Connect with
someone local.

Explore your questions
in a group.